Angie Nicolas

How to Open a Successful High-End Boutique

"A Great Coaching Guide on How to Run a Successful Boutique"

By Angie Nicolas © 2017

"How to open a successful High-End Boutique:
A Great Coaching Guide on How to Run a
Successful Boutique"

By Angie Nicolas © 2017

whatsoever for use or misuse of the information in this book.

ISBN-13:978-1541240384

ISBN-10:1541240383

Table of Content

Introduction

I will teach you how Turning an a-ha! moment into a success story. When I was a little girl I was the go to girl for fashion and style. I always knew how to pick great clothing and put them together to make statement pieces. In this book I will teach you HOW TO OWN YOUR OWN WORLD in the fashion business. I know your dream was always to be a BOSS. You are a fashionista. You want to start a boutique but don't know how. Let me help support your dream. Are you about to open a store or simply want some unbiased input on a store concept? This book will save you so much money on how to target the right resources. For example, this book will consult you, give your business advice, and help you save time from researching.

Did you know that in 2016 numbers for Retail Boutiques outlooks were growing at a quick rate? And that Global retail sales were $20 trillion in 2015 and are expected to reach $23 trillion in 2017. Research shows that analyst estimates put global sales close to $28 trillion by 2021. That is a growth worth investing into your own boutique. What I love about the industry is that private retailers employ over 28 million people.

Which includes direct and indirect employment such as software developers, security guards and marketing agents that number jumps to 42 million people by 2025? That is expected to generate some $1.2 trillion in labor income. The retail industry accounts for an average of 20% of jobs in every state. 40% of the retail workforce is employed at small businesses.

Just think in a few years you will be living the life you always wanted. Taking the vacation, buying your first home and driving the car of your dream. I know you will make the money you want by having work ethics, drive and following these concepts.

Starting a new business can be costly and time consuming; it requires a lot of dedication and effort. Owning your own world is the most fulfilling and rewarding thing you can ever do. If you are a person who loves to give up quickly when faced with challenges, this is not for you. If you are a go getter, empowered, full of energy, you are on your way. Even if you have experience or no experience in High End Boutique this book is for you. The numbers speak for themselves, success is around the corner, investing in yourself and building your business will aid in bringing you all you desire and aspire. I have owned my owned and operated my own boutique for more than 15 years. My personal credentials and techniques include costume design and wardrobe stylist. I'm very experienced, having been accustomed to set etiquette for many years. I have worked on a variety of films, some of which heavy in special effects which has brought out a deeper level of attention to detail for sake of continuity. I have styled e-commerce photo shoots for well-known companies. I've assisted on notable television companies with over 10 million watchers. Worked on projects such as Magazine Publishing companies as well. I am passionate about what I do and I am always committed to each project, storyline, and character that I am a part of developing.

As a successful High-End Boutique owner I am habitually ask, how did you do it, how did you get started. In this booked not only will I coach you, I will motivate and empower you during the process. Empowering you through this process is very important to me, because having the idea to open a business is one thing but having a support system is another, I will be your own personal cheerleader that will make you feel good. I remember as a kid I loved hearing one of my virtual mentor speaks the great American poet and author Maya Angelou, one of the most important figures in the American Civil Rights Movement, who said, "I've learned that people will forget what you said, people will forget what you did, but people will never forget how you made them feel. I will teach you the step by step and empower you to coach you along the way.

This book is for everyone and anyone searching on how to open and run a High-End Boutique, this book will take the time to explain how to start your business, how to market your business, and how to find distributors. Enjoy the Book!

CHAPTER 1- CREATING A NAME & BUSINESS PLAN

I have an intention for success and know it is a reality awaiting my arrival

The reason I finally decided to write a book, is because I get ask all the time, can you mentor me.

1) How much did it cost you to open?

2) How do you know what to sell?

3) Where do you get your inventory?

4) How do you know who's your client base?

5) Who decorated your store & How did you know which design fixtures to choose from?

As much as I love to help others my coaching mentor program for individuals can be very costly. This book will save you thousands of dollars.

When I opened my first storefront I called it "The Hot Spot 813". I was thinking BIG; I was thinking franchise I wasn't just thinking for now. The Hot Spot 813 is a High End Boutique store Thehotspot813.com We are premier in store & online shopping sanctuary that caters to women in search of the latest contemporary fashions and evening wear. Also offering a focused assortment of accessories, costume jewelry and emerging categories for stylish and savvy clientele, the main goal of the in store & e-retailer is to provide visitors with an easy one-stop shopping experience that will refine and rejuvenate one's wardrobe.

In this book I will also be your affirmation coach and help you understand the importance of believing in yourself. Opening a new business or an existing business can be an emotional rollercoaster. Especially during challenging times. Affirmations can be a powerful tool to help you change your mood, state of mind, and manifest the greatness you will see in your business. Make sure to write, speak, and visualize the things you seek. But they work best if you practice and believe in it. I want you to know this is very crucial to your success. A person's will is so powerful that it must be nurtured by constant repetition of positive self-talk. It serves as the engine for the human body to move and move faster.

I get ask all the time what is the purpose of having a Business Plan; my first thought comes from the quote of Lewis Carroll. In Alice's Adventures in Wonderland, Alice comes to a fork in the road and asks: "Would you tell me, please, which way I ought to go from here?" "That depends a good deal on where you want to get to," said the Cat. "I don't much care where–" said Alice. "Then it doesn't matter which way you go," said the Cat. Creating a Draft Outline for your business is very important, below is a sample draft you can draw from to help you plan how you want to structure your business. Again, this is just a draft, if you need more information you can refer with business consultant.

Executive Summary – You want to start out with a summary of your business. State facts about your business, you want to be unique, explain how you differ from other boutiques.

1.1 Objectives

In this section you will want to show your target audience. You can briefly explain who your business caters too; you can discuss market share, profit margins, and net profit.

1.2 Mission

In mission section, you explain your vision, your mission and the style you will be carrying in your store.

1.3 Keys to Success

Here you want to take the time to explain the assortment of inventory; you can discuss how you plan to target your audience.

Company Summary – In this section you want to confer how your business is formed, is it a Corporation, an LLC, or a Partnership. Discuss your ideal location or if you already have a store front you can add your address. Also, discuss your business focus.

2.1   Company Ownership

This section is self-explanatory; you discuss who or who owns the business.

2.2   Start-up Summary

Here you can input a summary of how you started your business. You can deliberate if the business has received a grant, if you have taken out a loan, if you have investors and so forth.

Table: Start-up

Items	Budget
Legal and Accounting	$1,000
Signage	$3,000
Telecom System	$80
Insurance	$350
Storefront Build-out	$30,000
Equipment	$4,000
Website Development	$2,000
Start-up Inventory	$10,000
Promotions	$2,000
Computer Systems	$1,750
Office Supplies	$875
Employee Salaries	$1,400
Security Systems	$200
Utilities	$500

Monthly Rent	$3,500
Monthly Events	$500
Total Requirements	$61,155

Table: Start-up Funding

Start-up Funding	
Start-up Assets	$150,000
Start-up Expenses	$61,155
Cash Balance After Start-Up	$88,845

2.3 Company Locations and Facilities

The section you can take the time to describe the dwellings of your business. Take the time and equip this section with every detail inside and out about your store.

Products — In this segment you can discuss how you plan to get your inventory. You can discuss if you plan to go directly to manufactures, or showrooms.

3.1 Product Description

For Product Description, you can list the types of brands you plan to carry, and how you plan on meeting your customer's needs.

3.2 Competitive Comparison

In this section you have the opportunity to show how you differ from your competition. You need to take the time to display your advantages over other boutiques in your area.

3.3 Sales Literature

This section has an opportunity for you to discuss the types of promotions you plan to display and different tools you can use for advertisement.

3.4 Sourcing

Sourcing is the section were you add all the sources you plan to use in order to purchase goods for your inventory. You can mention show rooms sources, manufactures, and vendors. If you are looking for sources, you can contact me directly at http://fashionnetworkingnightout.com/Boutique-Coaching

3.5 Technology

In the technology section, you can take the time to show the types of software, and computer systems. You can discuss the type of point of sales systems you will have, SKU's, and inventory control systems.

3.6 Future Products

For this segment, you can discuss the probability of adding additional products that you foresee you may need to continue to attract and dazzle clients. You can add details like adding a men's line in your boutique, or maybe even offering high-end pet clothing to supplement your market.

Market Segmentation- This section gives you an opportunity to divide your market into different sectors. You can discuss the types of groups you plan to focus on. You focus on the unique prospective buyers you plan to attract. Examples of market dissection can be found in the goods, publicizing and promotions that people use every day.

4.1 Target Market Segment Strategy

Every business and product needs to target a marketplace. In this section you want to explain how you plan on attracting different groups of customers and the several strategies to plan on using to attract them.

Examples:

- Neighborhood Storefront

- Friends & Customers (word of mouth and email)

- Personal shoppers and stylists

- Women's Fashion Magazines

- Local press mentions & ads

- Travel and shopping books and websites

Professional woman (ages 30-55)

- Household income over $100,00

- College-educated

- Lives in a higher-income neighborhood

4.2 Competition and Buying Patterns

This matter is still in the over-all range of describing the business. You can discuss what your keys to being successful are, what pricing range you plan to use.

Strategy and Implementation Summary – This section

gives you an opportunity to discuss the market share you plan to capture and the location you plan to have your business. You should take time to define a strategy that highlights your superiority in the market. For example, you can mention that you will develop strong relationships with customers by utilizing Style Assessment and offering services to help each woman determine the right clothes for her.

5.1 Competitive Edge

In this area you can show the type of advantage you will have over your competitors. You can compare the company strengths and weaknesses. Product specifications could be drawn up and show the competitive edge as well.

5.2 Marketing Strategy

For this area you can talk about your organizations strategy and combine all of your marketing goals into one comprehensive plan. The marketing strategy is the foundation of a marketing plan; you can spend time listing your brand positions.

BRAND PERSONALITY

Innovative | Stylish | Contemporary | Modern | Fresh | Approachable | Elegant

5.2.1 Pricing Strategy

In this section you can discuss the quality of your apparel, the types of product lines you will carry, and the retail price you plan use.

5.2.2 Promotion Strategy

Product promotion is one of the necessities for getting your brand in front of the public and attracting new customers.

5.2.3 Distribution Strategy

Distribution channels in marketing are a key element of your entire marketing strategy. A distribution channel helps you expand your reach & grow revenue.

5.2.4 Marketing Programs

A marketing program is a coordinated, thoughtfully designed
set of activities that help you achieve
your marketing objectives. Your marketing objectives are
strategic sales goals that fit your strengths and are a good way
to stretch your business in its current situation.

5.2.5 Positioning Statement

A positioning statement is a concise description of your target
market as well as a compelling picture of how you want that
market to perceive your brand.

5.3 Sales Strategy

A strategic sales plan is essential to the success of
your sales efforts. Without a good sales plan, sales success is
almost imposable. Your strategic plan should describe not just
your products and services, but your unique selling
proposition. Your USP is the thing that sets you apart from
your competition.

5.3.1 Sales Forecast

A sales forecast is an essential tool for managing a business of
any size. It is a month-by-month forecast of the level

of sales you expect to achieve. Most businesses draw up a sales forecast once a year.

Objective #1 - Sell $500,000 of merchandise in Year 1

Objective #2 - Generate 10% of Sales from Special Orders

Objective #3 - Garner In-Depth Understanding of Customers

Table: Sales Forecast

Sales Forecast			
	Year 1	Year 2	Year 3
Shoes	$109,000	$125,350	$144,153
Jewelry	$80,000	$92,000	$105,800
Clothing	$220,000	$253,000	$290,000
Hats & Belts	$43,840	$50,416	$57,979
Subtotal Direct Cost of Sales	$452,840	$520,766	$539,953

5.4 Milestones

Business milestones are like checkpoints for entrepreneurs, signaling that a business venture is thriving and growing. Milestones are the events that occur on the way toward achieving the desired end results of business goals. They can be short- or long-term goals and can be easily achievable or challenging.

Table: Milestones

Milestones					
Milestone	Start Date	End Date	Budget	Manager	Department
Policies	12/1/2016	5/1/2017	$0		Executive
Lease	12/1/2016	7/1/2017	$0		Business Development

	12/1/2016	11/1/2017	$0		Finance
Totals			$0		

Management Summary- When writing business plans, it is important to spend time writing your company's management summary. Many times, investors will choose to invest in a company solely on the strength of the management team. ... The ideal management summary emphasizes your specific responsibilities, positions, and previous successes.

6.1 Organizational Structure

An organizational structure describes how actions such as task allocation, organization and supervision are directed toward the accomplishment of organizational goals. It can also be considered as the viewing glass or outlook through which individuals see their organization and its atmosphere.

6.2 Management Team

The management team is an essential part of every business. This team analyzes and identifies the business' goals and objectives and implements and enforces the strategies the employees need to achieve success. In a business plan, the management team includes the business' owners, board of directors and managers.

6.3 Personnel Plan

In many companies one of the biggest costs of doing business is the staff (employees) and related expenses. In this section you can discuss the plans you have with your employees and the roles they present.

Table: Personnel

Personnel Plan			
	Year 1	Year 2	Year 3
Owner	$48,000	$52,000	$60,000
Manager	$27,500	$30,000	$33,000
Team Lead	$17,500	$20,000	$23,000
Sales agent	$11,520	$13,040	$16,040
Total People	4	4	4
Total Payroll	$104,520	$115,040	$132,040

Financial Plan- The purpose of the financial section of a business plan is two-fold. You're going to need it if you are seeking investment from venture capitalists, angel investors, or even family members.

7.1 Break-even Analysis

The Break-even Analysis calculates what will be needed in monthly revenue to reach the break-even point. Cost of goods for the break-even are based on line sheets from the vendors that you plan to carry. In addition, try to plan to maintain an average 60% retail markup to maintain sales revenues well above the break-even level noted below.

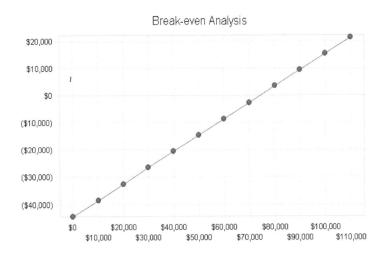

Table: Break-even Analysis

Break-even Analysis	
Monthly Revenue Break-even	$48,808
Assumptions:	
Average Percent Variable Cost	20%
Estimated Monthly Fixed Cost	$29,285

7.2 Projected Profit and Loss

The following table presents projected profit and loss.

	Year 1	Year 2	Year 3	Year 4	Year 5
TOTAL SALES	$513,503	$599,403	$609,402	$620,315	$630,937
Casual Tops	$20,588	$23,774	$24,012	$24,614	$24,983
Blouses	$17,370	$20,176	$20,378	$20,889	$21,202
Sweaters	$15,684	$18,272	$18,455	$18,918	$19,202
Knits	$16,447	$18,973	$19,163	$19,643	$19,938
Pants	$17,483	$20,288	$20,491	$21,005	$21,320
Skirts	$13,874	$16,200	$16,362	$16,773	$17,024
Dresses	$9,922	$11,670	$11,787	$12,082	$12,263
Denim	$11,990	$14,155	$14,296	$14,655	$14,874
Separates	$8,010	$9,436	$9,531	$9,770	$9,916
Jackets/Blazers	$10,689	$12,759	$12,886	$13,209	$13,408
Coats/Outerwear	$7,996	$9,454	$9,548	$9,788	$9,934
Fashion Accessories	$18,680	$21,466	$21,681	$22,225	$22,558
Jewelry	$7,998	$9,346	$9,440	$9,676	$9,821
Personal Care	$4,793	$5,666	$5,722	$5,866	$5,954
Wardrobe Accessories	$7,095	$8,413	$8,497	$8,710	$8,841
Style Assessment	$1,107	$1,179	$1,191	$1,221	$1,239
Special Orders	$14,500	$15,655	$15,812	$16,208	$16,451
Alterations	$596	$638	$644	$660	$670
Subtotal Direct Cost of Sales	$204,820	$237,520	$239,896	$245,911	$249,600

Table: Profit and Loss

Pro Forma Profit and Loss	Year 1	Year 2	Year 3
Sales	$452,840	$520,766	$539,953

Direct Cost of Sales	$176,729	$286,906	$328,751
Other Production Expenses	$0	$0	$0
Total Cost of Sales	$176,729	$286,906	$328,751
Gross Margin	$276,111	$233,860	$211,202
Gross Margin %	60.00%	60.00%	60.00%
Expenses			
Payroll	$104,520	$115,040	$132,040
Sales and Marketing and Other Expenses	$8,400	$8,400	$8,400
Depreciation	$1,704	$1,704	$1,704
Leased Equipment	$0	$0	$0
Utilities	$4,800	$4,800	$4,800
Insurance	$3,600	$3,600	$3,600
Rent	$24,000	$24,000	$24,000
Payroll Taxes	$40,293	$48,444	$49,644
Other	$0	$0	$0
Net Profit	$187,047	$205,988	$224,188

7.3 Projected Cash Flow

The following chart and table display the projected cash flow.

Chart: Cash

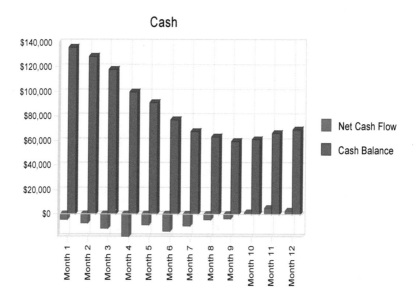

Table: Cash Flow

Pro Forma Cash Flow	Year 1	Year 2	Year 3
Cash Received			
Cash from Operations			
Cash Sales	$452,840	$520,766	$539,953
Subtotal Cash from Operations	$452,840	$520,766	$539,953
Additional Cash Received			
Sales Tax, VAT, HST/GST Received	$0	$0	$0
New Current Borrowing	$0	$0	$0
New Other Liabilities (interest-free)	$0	$0	$0

New Long-term Liabilities	$0	$0	$0
Sales of Other Current Assets	$0	$0	$0
Sales of Long-term Assets	$0	$0	$0
New Investment Received	$0	$0	$0
Subtotal Cash Received	$452,840	$520,766	$539,953
Cash Spending	$268,620	$322,960	$330,960
Bill Payments	$244,177	$564,066	$551,685
Subtotal Spent on Operations	$512,797	$887,026	$882,645
Additional Cash Spent			
Sales Tax, VAT, HST/GST Paid Out	$0	$0	$0
Principal Repayment of Current Borrowing	$0	$0	$0
Other Liabilities Principal Repayment	$0	$0	$0
Long-term Liabilities Principal Repayment	$0	$0	$0
Purchase Other Current Assets	$0	$0	$0
Purchase Long-term Assets	$0	$0	$0
Dividends	$0	$0	$0
Subtotal Cash Spent	$512,797	$887,026	$882,645
Net Cash Flow	($70,975)	$80,239	$189,232
Cash Balance	$69,525	$149,765	$338,997

7.4 Important Assumptions

The following table details important financial assumptions.

Table: General Assumptions

General Assumptions			
	Year 1	Year 2	Year 3
Plan Month	1	2	3
Current Interest Rate	10.00%	10.00%	10.00%
Long-term Interest Rate	10.00%	10.00%	10.00%
Tax Rate	30.00%	30.00%	30.00%
Other	0	0	0

7.5 Projected Balance Sheet

The following table shows the projected balance sheet.

Table: Balance Sheet

Pro Forma Balance Sheet			
	Year 1	Year 2	Year 3
Assets			
Current Assets			
Cash	$69,525	$149,765	$338,997
Inventory	$28,838	$81,940	$45,962
Other Current Assets	$0	$0	$0
Total Current Assets	$98,364	$231,704	$384,958
Long-term Assets			
Long-term Assets	$8,500	$8,500	$8,500
Accumulated Depreciation	$1,704	$3,408	$5,112
Total Long-term Assets	$6,796	$5,092	$3,388
Total Assets	$105,160	$236,796	$388,346
Liabilities and Capital	Year 1	Year 2	Year 3
Current Liabilities			
Accounts Payable	$32,484	$47,604	$45,142
Current Borrowing	$0	$0	$0
Other Current Liabilities	$0	$0	$0
Subtotal Current Liabilities	$32,484	$47,604	$45,142
Long-term Liabilities	$0	$0	$0
Total Liabilities	$32,484	$47,604	$45,142
Paid-in Capital	$183,100	$183,100	$183,100
Retained Earnings	($24,100)	($110,424)	$6,092
Earnings	($86,324)	$116,516	$154,013
Total Capital	$72,676	$189,192	$343,205
Total Liabilities and Capital	$105,160	$236,796	$388,346

Net Worth	$72,676	$189,192	$343,205

The following table shows the projected business ratios

Table: Ratios

Ratio Analysis				
	Year 1	Year 2	Year 3	Industry Profile
Sales Growth	n.a.	118.93%	10.82%	11.07%
Percent of Total Assets				
Inventory	27.42%	34.60%	11.84%	36.78%
Other Current Assets	0.00%	0.00%	0.00%	26.80%
Total Current Assets	93.54%	97.85%	99.13%	90.26%
Long-term Assets	6.46%	2.15%	0.87%	9.74%
Total Assets	100.00%	100.00%	100.00%	100.00%
Current Liabilities	30.89%	20.10%	11.62%	45.28%
Long-term Liabilities	0.00%	0.00%	0.00%	14.93%
Total Liabilities	30.89%	20.10%	11.62%	60.21%
Net Worth	69.11%	79.90%	88.38%	39.79%
Percent of Sales				
Sales	100.00%	100.00%	100.00%	100.00%
Gross Margin	60.00%	60.00%	60.00%	14.44%
Selling, General & Administrative Expenses	93.39%	44.47%	42.20%	2.35%
Advertising Expenses	1.28%	0.50%	0.45%	0.38%
Profit Before Interest and Taxes	-19.54%	17.21%	20.53%	1.99%
Main Ratios				
Current	3.03	4.87	8.53	1.74
Quick	2.14	3.15	7.51	0.86
Total Debt to Total Assets	30.89%	20.10%	11.62%	63.63%
Pre-tax Return on Net Worth	-118.78%	87.98%	64.11%	5.59%
Pre-tax Return on Assets	-82.09%	70.29%	56.66%	15.37%

Additional Ratios	Year 1	Year 2	Year 3	
Net Profit Margin	-19.54%	12.05%	14.37%	n.a
Return on Equity	-118.78%	61.59%	44.87%	n.a
Activity Ratios				
Inventory Turnover	10.34	6.99	6.70	n.a
Accounts Payable Turnover	8.52	12.17	12.17	n.a
Payment Days	27	25	31	n.a
Total Asset Turnover	4.20	4.08	2.76	n.a
Debt Ratios				
Debt to Net Worth	0.45	0.25	0.13	n.a
Current Liab. To Liab.	1.00	1.00	1.00	n.a
Liquidity Ratios				
Net Working Capital	$65,880	$184,100	$339,817	n.a
Interest Coverage	0.00	0.00	0.00	n.a
Additional Ratios				
Assets to Sales	0.24	0.24	0.36	n.a
Current Debt/Total Assets	31%	20%	12%	n.a
Acid Test	2.14	3.15	7.51	n.a
Sales/Net Worth	6.08	5.11	3.12	n.a
Dividend Payout	0.00	0.00	0.00	n.a

Starting a business is a thrilling proposal, but it's also an extremely thought-provoking undertaking. Your business plan will help you map your future, and help you secure funding from investors if needed. Your business plan can also address the next phase in the development process.

CHAPTER 2 - THE IMPORTANCE OF A GREAT LOCATION

***Building my business to serve others is my desire. ***

When opening a High End Boutique, the location is very important. The location is a big part of contributing in to the success of the business; you must choose a spot accordingly. Launching a BOUTIQUE, don't let the lure of low rent tempt you into a lease deal. This can kill your business before it ever gets off the ground. Trust me I know. The purpose of it is to make sure you understand that investing in the location is very imperative, because the wrong location can cause the business to fail. If you have a lower budget that you are working with don't allow the low rent draw you in. This can kill your business before it ever gets off the ground. Make sure to choose a lease according to the demographic of the clientele you are looking for.

Your main goal is to have foot traffic when opening a boutique. Don't let a higher lease or rent payment scare you. If a location truly offers prime foot-traffic, walk-ins and easy access for your customers, it may be well worth the investment. Make sure you understand that your lease is simply part of your overall marketing spending to get people in the door. Here are some other great tips to consider when searching for a great location.

Make sure to have a great relationship with your Real estate agent, make sure your agent is one who understands your overall needs and would fight for you in getting the best deal as possible. Here are some things to also consider. It will benefit your business to be around similar businesses that are already drawing the type of customers that you want, a great example; my boutique was always in a downtown area, where it attracted snow birds and tourist. There was no doubt that you will get profit from being near comparable shops. Since many people are shopping for clothes, they tend to spend several hours in a shopping district.

Another great tip to look at before choosing a retail store location is to define how you see your business, both now and in the future.

- Who are your client bases?
- Can you really see yourself & Business in this space?
- The type of High End Products you're selling is this a great area for it? Look at yourself from your client's perspective.
- Do you prefer to be at a shopping center?
- Can a mall setting be more ideal?
- Have you determined how much retail space, storage area, and the size of the office space you need?

I want you to understand therefore you don't confuse a lot of traffic for a lot of customers. Many boutiques want to be located where they can have their target audience.

- How many people walk or drive past the location?
- Is the area served by public transportation?
- Can customers and delivery trucks easily get in and out of the parking lot?
- Is there adequate parking?

These questions are very important in finding your ideal location space. Since I always had my boutique in a downtown location, it was very challenging and rewarding at the same time. Some of the challenges I experienced was difficulty for clients to find parking. Especially for new clients. It can really be a turn off for some. Since it was so difficult to find parking I offered my clients valet services. I was able to offer the valet service by partnering with several valet services near me. I hope this situation has brought to light some issues may have when finding the ideal location.

Before signing a lease makes sure you understand the long term commitment you will have between you and your landlord. I advise that in order to run a successful Boutique your lease must be at minimum 3 years' maximum of 5 years'. The reason being, it will take time to build up your clientele base and make a name for yourself and your company. But the most important take away is to make sure you have a real estate attorney look over your lease before signing. It is extremely vital to do that. The reason why this is so important is many people will hire an attorney to fix a problem not to prevent the problem.

Once things have gone wrong in a transaction, you will often have to pay a substantial amount of attorneys' fees as a result. It is more beneficial, and less costly, to hire an attorney to protect you before a problem arises. Also, if a dispute ascends, one of the biggest mistakes clients make is not contacting an attorney soon enough. In my state the Florida law is very specific as to landlord / tenant law and it is important you understand and follow such in your lease contract.

The most common issues that create disputes with lease agreements include:

1. Condition of the property was not thoroughly investigated.
2. Unclear language concerning the responsible party for maintenance and repairs.
3. Unclear language as to the type and amount of insurance required to be obtained by each party.

4. Notice and cure periods, as well as when late fees are triggered, or are not clearly stated.

5. The language is not clear as to how the tenant may exercise an option for the lease term to be extended, known as a renewal option, nor does the lease clearly provide the rent for the renewal option and what happens if the parties cannot agree upon the new rent amount.

6. The lease was not signed as required by law or an authorized representative did not sign the lease.

7. Language does not address who owns alterations or improvements made to the property.

8. Unclear language as to if either party is obligated to repair or rebuild in event of partial or total destruction, or when a party has the right to terminate the lease in the event of destruction.

9. Failure to clearly state the conditions to be satisfied for the security deposit to be returned to tenant.

10. If tenant is given an option to purchase, the language fails to clearly provide the terms and conditions of said option and whether tenant's deposit for the option is non-refundable. I contemplate that number #10 is very significant.

Your business might be doing very well and now you have the extra cash to buy the property where it can save you thousands of dollars. Ownership is very important because it will give you more room for future improvement and expansions.

Finally, I want you to take this very serious and understand that commercial landlords should avoid using a previously-prepared lease agreement for a new transaction, even if the agreement was prepared by an attorney. Not only is each transaction unique, but the laws may have changed since the drafting of the previous agreement. I want you to understand once a dispute arises with a lease agreement, the attorney must work within the language in the lease agreement and that may cost you monetarily, especially a new business who are not in the profit margin yet. You can avoid other future problems or effects being handled more expeditiously, if the lease clearly and concisely sets forth the terms of the agreement. HIRING AN ATTORNEYIS is a great tip for your business succeeding. A great example of signing a bad lease was when I thought I met the greatest landlord, the energy was right I understood the lease. But then I soon realize it was the lease from hell. When the boutique had a sewer leakage with a burst pipe from the outside ground. I was legally responsible to fix it. When the AC stops working I had to replace it. This situation caused so much battle so

much tension between me and my landlord. He had no inclination to assist. He would often remind me I am in a binding contract and I was

legally responsible for it. Then I re-read the lease. I was responsible for everything, even if the roof falls off. This scenario causes so much

negative emotions for myself and employees, because all the profit that was being made went to paying more than $9,000.00 in cost to fix the plumbing. It was a lesson that I would never forget.

Also before signing your lease make sure to negotiate several months' free rent depending on the condition of the store front. It may take about 60-120 days to complete the build out so you want to negotiate FREE rent for the time the space being renovated. Keep in mind; you can negotiate content to include in the lease that your landlord assists with build out process.

After you have your location and lease in order, you will need to apply for your city and state business license. It is preferable to set up appointments or walk in to apply instead of going online. When in person, you have the opportunity to make connections with the Chamber of Commerce officials. Remember without your licenses you will not be able to order inventory's from the wholesalers, because having your licenses is curtailing to them selling to you and allowing you to re-sell. Depending on what's state and city you're in, you will need a sales tax id in order to have more than one employee. Contact the board of Equalization, IRS and Employee Development Departments for more information. During this process you want to open a business checking account. When I opened my business I joined my local chamber, they were very supportive with my type of business, and if your Boutique is in downtown area, I would join the downtown devolvement, it is a free service for all small business with free advertisement and events that your business can be a part of. Make use of they have to offer, these options are there for you to win and help build your new business.

CHAPTER 3- VISUAL DESIGN & BRANDING

I DESERVE ABUNDANCE AND PROSPERITY

Now that you have chosen your space, I would like to be the first to congratulate you for taking the first plunge of becoming a successful entrepreneur. Designing your Boutique is a vital tool on the success of your store and a great opportunity to bring more clients into your store. Try to look at your store from the client's perspective. Remember your clients only have a few seconds to view and be attracted by your displays. First impressions matter. When it comes to fashion, impressions matter the most. As a store owner it's up to you to ensure your merchandise is displayed in an attractive, engaging manner in order to create a buzz to motivate clients to make a purchase. Designing your store can be as simple or as complex as you want it to be. When executed correctly, it will help convey the image of your brand and reflect the target market that your store wants to attract. So keep in mind when designing a storefront your clients will be your walking billboard, they will spread the word on the experience they had at your boutique. They will let the world know if you're Hot or if you're NOT. My advice to you is to drive around to different boutiques and even attend local trade shows. What you see will tell a story and create a lifestyle to the clienteles you wish to seek.

Let's talk about why is it so critical to put in time, effort and money in decorating your High End Boutique. Exclusive boutiques specialize in bags, high end clothing and fashionable accessories. As boutiques vary in their offerings, it is tough to identify explicit ideas as to decorations. However, there are selected decorating ideas that will work in all boutiques, at any degree.

Lighting: This is a must when opening a boutique. To have an incredible an irresistible shop and to be able to showcase to your future cliental, you must start with specialty lighting designed to attract and engage the high-end shopper looking for luxury, elegance and expensive merchandise. Your boutique will need a perfect combination of functional, aesthetic and mood lighting. To create a more pleasant atmosphere, you should try to partially hide the ambient light fixtures with louvers or baffles as this will put more attention on the merchandise. Put the accent light fixtures as close as you can to the products. You can also add attention to key areas of the store by using exposed or decorative accent light fixtures. Lighting is very important to have the degree of lighting in your store will vary depending on the mood you desire to create. If you set up your light fixtures properly, they will greatly enhance the atmosphere of your store and help boost your sales.

Color: Colors can make or break your whole theme. Make sure to choose your color scheme to correspond to your boutique image. The colors of the Boutique wall and the overall Boutique color ideas you utilize will also play an important role in whether or not the customer will make a purchase. The color you chose gives a sort of inviting feel. If choosing a color is hard keep, there are other options, like adding a wallpaper to give the shop a great blend. I remember the excitement I had when designing my boutique. I chose wall paper it gave me the signature iconic looks for my overall cliental. One of my favorite wallpaper brands is the PHILLIP JEFFRIES (Quilted Lacquer). Remember color creates a powerful emotional and visual stimulus. Keep in mind that the colors you chose for the space will influence your clients buying habits as well as your employee's productivity.

Designing & Furniture: When I designed my boutique I kept in mind that I was a specialty store that specializes in selling High-End type of merchandise, in my boutiques we specialized in evening wear, like Galas, homecoming, prom and more. The styles will not sell themselves though; they need to be showcased in a shop with a design as alluring as its clientele. Depending on your sketch layouts, generally you must show the size and location of each department, any permanent structures, fixture locations and customer traffic patterns. Come up with a theme for your shop or an atmosphere that you wish to create. Keep your targeted clientele in mind when brainstorming. Another great idea is to remember that in order to create a cozier, luxurious feeling in your boutique store show your product lines in unique ways. Here is an

example, Hang a few pieces in an antique armoire. Another great example is to place a small dresser in the corner and leave the top drawer wide open to showcase your products such as accessories or jewelry. Keep in mind some clients do not shop alone, they sometime have friends and friends with them. It is great idea to have your comfortable chairs around for guest to sit and relax. An antique chaise lounge, bench with cushions and other unique chairs will dress up your boutique. I had a chair in the middle of my showroom with a wine bar with complimentary drinks.

Interior layout: When laying out your boutiques it

is a must that you have a free-form layout so customers meandering around the racks of clothing or shop's perimeter. You can also divide your boutique area into separate sections like greeting and transaction area. Use the boutique's size to your advantage by creating an intimate atmosphere. When choosing your flooring you must add quality carpet or wood flooring it will create a more inviting feel than plain tile, make sure the interior has distinct touches. When purchasing furniture and decorations for your boutique keep in mind that you are selling clothing and not art or furniture, so these items should not be distracting in any way. Furniture should be comfortable, and inviting to encourage your customers to spend more time in your boutique. Avoid straight aisle ways that block other areas of the store from view. Smaller, round racks combined with displays around the store's perimeter encourage the clients to continued browse. This will help to make the shop more cohesive and create a memorable experience for the customer, last but not least when decorating tries to coordinate your theme with the name of your boutique.

CHAPTER 4 - INVENTORY MANAGEMENT & TRADESHOW COACHING

"Overcoming my fears to move in the direction of my dreams."

Congratulations again, by this point you should have your Seller's Permit and your Business License. Remember, you may not be able to get all the lines that you want. After you have your Seller's Permit and Business License, make a list of brands that you would like to carry. Here is more information from my own experience, when shopping for your boutique it is imperative that you understanding your demographic. This is a very important part of your business, it will save you a lot of time once you decided who your audience is, it will also help you identify the style of clothing that will best fit your audience and be profitable. At The Hot Spot 813 Boutique our niche was to cater to women with a particular lifestyle, Doctors, Lawyers, Board members, charity organizations and believe it or not High school seniors.

Finding wholesalers for your particular clientele, doesn 't necessarily mean "cheap." Because I always tell a client to choose quality over quantity especially owning a one of a kind boutique. There are two things that everyone needs to consider; Quantity vs. Quality. Unfortunately, the two don't normally go hand-in-hand. I would recommend that you buy locally in USA, making a trip out to LA and try the fashion district there. Atlanta Mart, Las Vegas, Chicago. The reason being is that the major cities tend to have all the upcoming trends and style. I would also consider going to Fashion week it is a great way to stay connected with the fashion world so you can get a visual of the upcoming season. Another great reason to attend, you must start to learn to collaborate with other entrepreneurs like yourself. Consider it as mentoring each other. I love the quote that says "Birds of a feather flocks together". You want to be around people who will take you higher, so don't feel intimidated by other entrepreneurs like yourself in this industry there is room for all of us to grow.

Here is some information on buying recommendations. Understand that these big companies have daily shows from different lineups. Check their schedules for details. Tips for shopping a trade show. The point of all this is to meet vendors whose merchandise you may want to carry.

You also can make direct purchases at trade shows such as MAGIC, a fashion trade show that occurs twice a year in Las Vegas or the twice yearly New York International Gift Fair. You can also develop a relationship with overseas artist, you can order directly from them through the Internet or other avenues of communication.

• Register early and online.

• Start your day early.

• Pick up the trade show book and map out your day.

• Walk row by row.

• You can leave your orders at the show but make sure to mark them, "hold for confirmation".

• Bring a notebook, stapler and an extra pair of shoes.

Magic International: (818) 593-5000

Los Angeles Mart: (213) 683-8484

Atlanta Mart: (888) 263-7456

When shopping for inventory makes sure you understand the math in buying and in reselling. Build relationships with vendors and get your name added to mailing lists so you can learn of new products and special deals as they appear. If you can, travel abroad and look for unique clothes, jewelry and gifts to purchase from local artist that would stand out in your boutique. I want you to know when you're a smaller Boutique, you must understand when thinking of inventory in terms weeks of supply is a new concept, you can easily think about inventory in terms of quantity, in terms of units, cases or case packs, as well as how much inventory you need to build an effective display.

Make sure you understand what return on investment means, but in managing the day to day urgencies of your business, this is also crucial time to focus on sales, believing that maximizing sales will lead to positive cash flow. However, what I did at my boutique was instinctively focus on how much I might be able to sell. I would not keep inventory past a season, I would focus on keeping the latest up with the latest trends and selling off inventory to other boutiques, or offer bulk deals at trunk shows. Unless you can quantify the number of weeks of supplies that you have on hand, and the number of additional weeks of supply that you are purchasing, you will have no way of projecting when you can expect to sell that inventory and convert it into cash. I will give you hands on examples of what that can mean for you and your new business. As much as excitement you may have, you must take this process very seriously

• <u>Mark-Up (Margin)</u>: Following the manufactures standards. Then charging the most you can for the product

• <u>Turn-Over</u>: Understanding the turn-over is literally how many times goods get restocked. Total net sales for the year = Turnover Average inventory at retail $60,000 / $5,000 = 12.0 turns per year

• <u>Sales to Stock Ratio</u>: Sales to Stock Ratio: The amount of stock you have on hand in relation to the sales you are predicting. Inventory on hand at the beginning of the month at retail = Sales to stock Ratio Amount of predicted sales 90,000 in inventory/ 30,000 predicted sales = 3/1

- <u>Sales per Square foot</u>: Projected Yearly sales (or yearly sales) =Sales per square foot Total sq. feet of selling space

- <u>O.T.B (Open to Buy):</u> If, you have to sell $20,000 a month to meet your overhead you would take your average price point, let's say it is $30, and divide it by the $20,000.

- <u>R.O.I (Return on Investment)</u>
ROI= Understand that every dollar you put in the return of your Investment the amount of profit, before taxes and after depreciation from the investment made.

CHAPTER 5- BRANDING & RETAIL MARKETING STRATEGY

"A brand is the set of expectations, memories, stories and relationships that, taken together, account for a consumer's decision to choose one product or service over another"

When I was in the branding process of my stores, the first thing that came on my mind was lifestyle with a great presentation for my future shoppers. As a small business owner I believe that my business serves a need for a particular audience. When building your brand, you need to know what your brand equals or what you want it to equal. Write down all the characteristics that describe what you are and how you would like to be perceived. This is very important to understand, because I believe perception becomes reality. In branding your boutiques this one of the most important aspects to understand.

Once you compile that list in what you are looking to be perceived as, you could fine-tune it and make sure you have full command of your brand in order to reach your customers and, more importantly, your potential cliental. Branding yourself effectively is important because people purchase on emotion, people are seeking an image, which is why your own image is crucial as well to the success of the store. The images and style, not only in the products you sell but also for the customers who wear your clothing pieces. Branding is an integral part of positioning your company as a popular source of world-class that will help your customers look better and gain confidence in their own images. This very simply if you do it right. Understand that your brand is your promise to your customer. It tells them what they can expect from your products and services; it differentiates you and your competitors'.

Your brand is copy from who you are, who you want to be and who people perceive you to be. As a business owner your brand is essentially everything. It ensures they will recall your boutique when they're searching for something specific or when a friend or family member is asking for advice about where to shop, your brand will recreate a BUZZ on itself to the type of feeling you want your customer to have when they're thinking about you and your shop.

What is your mission statement? This process is like a self-discovering. Learn it believe it in.

- What do your customers and prospects already think of your company?

- What qualities do you want them to associate with your company?

Make sure to create a "voice" for your BOUTIQUE that creates an imagery that reflects your brand. This voice should be applied to all written communication and incorporated in the visual imagery of all materials, online and off. When I built boutique I wanted it to have a voice. I wanted the words to says, Conservative, high class, Rich and expensive. I also wanted it to feel and act likes an individual that the people wanted to hang around. My boutique was always the place where you see quality rather than quantity. A place you can trust and deliver world class excellence in service and products.

Now let's talk about marketing your company, I believe in Sometimes the best way to get noticed is by doing things the old-fashioned way. When your consumers are fans of your brand and identify with it, they may become vocal in spreading your brand's message. Word of mouth marketing has always been important. Having a satisfied customer after each sales and spreading the word is like a walking billboards. You can offer a customer ambassador reward perks for each client they draw in after purchase and referrals. Making your clients feel good about themselves when leaving the shop and giving special treatments it will motivate them to promote your products and services. Their endorsement may be more powerful than any commercial or copy you could produce.

When I was a little girl, I remember hearing that birds of a feather flock together. So having the right shopper to advocate your brand and store, it will help marketing the voice and message to their friends, family on becoming new clients for your shop. Remember a strong group of caretakers of your brand may lead to further reaching brand ambassadors with your consumers. When you build that consistency and integrity and it flows through your customers, you just may hit a Brand Glam Ambassador. When marketing your shop. Make sure you use the same color scheme, logo placement, look and feel throughout and be very consistent. Another great way to market yourself is collaborating with local organizations, chose one that meets and aligned with the cliental you are looking for. Like empowering women's groups. They normally have a certain type of membership requirements that will be suitable for your future buyers. I would definitely become a member and when you do, you can have organized future fashion shows that will help you to market your products. I would also look into charities volunteering your time to non-profit organization women's expos it will help build future clients.

This system helped me saved so much money when I first started. It helped me in branding and name recognition to the community that my shops were in. I would also carry business cards with you. Give them freely and ask permission to leave them in places your target audience. Use an answering machine or voice mail system to catch after-hours phone calls. Include basic information in your outgoing messages such as business hours, location, website, etc.

Creating a Press release is very important to let the world know you mean business. Advertise in creative locations such as park benches, buses, and popular Web sites. For example, I advertise with my local community magazine, when I did, it created

creditability. Create a Newsletter and email marketing this is a key in keeping in touch with the customers you have managed to get in your store or on your website. It takes a lot of work to gain a customer. So make sure you find ways to stay connected. Like in some of my emails marketing campaigned, I would offer, bonuses, when they shop with you. For example, my loyal clients get 10% off every time they shop. They get inclusive invitation to events and new merchandise. It is very important to be vocal in your business. I would look into social media, Social media is one of the easiest, most cost effective things you can do. Make sure that you have a steady stream of activity online, one of my favorites that shows
great branding is Twitter, Instagram, Snapchat and Facebook.

In this day in age everyone is using the internet. As a business it is very important to stay connect to your customers, make sure they see a flurry of activity from you. Not seeing frequent activity at periods and silence it will speak volume that you are only online because sales are down.

Use social media to position yourself as the place to shop and buy new and existing inventory with confidence and desirable place to shop.

Another great place to market yourself is through your local newspaper ads, magazines, specialty publications and other forms of marketing. One great way to do this is to use remnant advertising. These are spaces in the paper that are "holes" for the local newspaper. You simply create a branding ad that the newspaper can drop in at its discretion. Make sure its catchy for example, for my couture boutique store, my ad had a headline that said "Are you a fashionista, are your prom ready? We can help." We got a ton of traffic off of that ad. The key, though, make sure its sales motivate and branding a presence to your shop. The most important thing is to keep the momentum going. Another great marketing tool is to get Endorse for local celebrities. Look into your favorite celebrity and reach out to them, follow them, make sure to be intentional by liking their stuff. Create a contractual agreement where you can send them products weekly. Once they like your stuff. Depending on how many followers that they have they will celebrate with you to their fans and followers. So make sure to choose a celebrity that will add market value to your future cliental. I've worked with so many celebrities that help shape the direction wanted to take my shop. In everything you do have the confidence level to make sure you get my yes to different Celebs agreeing to endorse your products.

The Hot Spot 813

CHAPTER 6- GRAND OPENING EVENT PLANNING

Angie Nicolas motto is "Presentation is everything"

Oh my goodness, this is your big day. I want to congratulate you on your new beginning. I want to be the first to wish you the best in your new boutique. I hope the contents of this book help guide, shape and set the bar high for your success. Part of having great success in your business is to have a level of self-confidence it will help you in so many ways like your behavior, your body language, how you speak, what you say, and so on. The reason why I am saying this is because you are your brand, in order for people to believe in you, you must believe in yourself. Confident people inspire confidence in others: their audience, their peers, their customers, and their friends. People who lack self-confidence can find it difficult to become successful, most people are reluctant to buy what you are selling. Make sure you are not nervous, fumbling, or overly apologetic, make sure to position yourself ass the boss that you are. DO NOT QUIT. Remember that anything worth having is worth working hard for. There were times that I lost my focus and my confidence, its shows through the store performances. Make sure you focus on growth and the strength you have in your shop.

Make sure you do not talk yourself out of your dream. Consistency and trusting in yourself will bring confidence. Above all, remember you are capable and worthy just as much as anyone else, regardless of what you've achieved. Believing it is the key to living it. And living it is the key to reaching your potential. Now that we establish the understanding on your new founding to success, I am sending you love and prosperity with so much success. Now it's time to party. I will provide you with step by step information of your opening so that way you can keep your future clients talking about you and knowing what they can expect when shopping with you.

Your grand opening event should be defined by a set of goals. This opening will embark what you want people to know about you and where you are located, and what you offer. You want to get people talking about you. You want to build relationships with local officials and potential clients. The first thing I would do is to join your local chamber. This is very critical because they will bring about 5-20 people with them who are already members. They will become your new found support system. Please note that Customers aren't the only people that will attend your unveiling. A grand opening opens up the potential to showcase your product to potential clients, business partners, investors, suppliers, and vendors. Grand openings can be a major source of publicity. It's a prime time to network and build relationships within the community.

Remember, not everyone will be able to attend your event, so it's just as important for people to hear about the grand opening as it is for them to attend the grand opening. If they hear about it, there's a good chance they will think about your store the next time they need something. When you join your local chamber they already have a database full of members, with this they will send out an email blast to all announcing your opening. Even if all don't show up, the buzz is there and they will remember to visit you when time permits.

The more information you have out there about your opening like, press, emails, and local paper, it will help others talk about you and business around town. The more you are on their minds and the more they will remember you the next time they need your specific products.

A successful grand opening evokes excitement and curiosity. The grand opening is your first big marketing push. You want to reach attendees through advertisements, promotions, local press coverage and word-of-mouth, you want to whole town knowing about you. Fortunately, the words "Grand Opening" themselves carry a lot of buzz. You just have to make sure they reach a big audience! Grand openings are the perfect opportunity to build relationships with local business people, press and local politicians. Not only do you get started on the right foot with your neighbors, but you can build strategic relationships, too.

Here is what you will need to know in order to have a successful grand opening. Please make sure you have the following before the day of the grand opening. You never want to apologies for not having something in store. The worst thing you can do at your grand opening is not being fully prepared to receive your customers.

- Signs
- Shelves
- Clothing Racks
- Hangers
- Point-of-Sale Solution
- Cash Register
- Bags
- Display Cases
- Rotating Racks
- Mirrors
- Mannequins
- Specialty Displays
- Stickers
- Receipt Paper or Printer
- Security System

Its Grand Opening Day!

Cue the balloons, sound the trumpets, and roll out the red carpet. After months of slaving away to make your dream a reality, the time has finally come to welcome your throngs of new customers. Let the celebration planning begins. While you have carefully planned the day out for your event, here are something's you want to think about: The Arrival: Who will be greeting visitors? What options or information should you be providing visitors when they arrive? The Visit: Do you expect everyone to arrive at once or sporadically? Do you have smaller events or activities planned for visitors who arrive early? The Departure: Are you giving visitors parting gifts (for example: free t-shirts, key chain, or a gift bag)? Are you going to try to get visitors to join your mailing list or become a Facebook fan before they leave? In meanwhile, make sure to have Drinks, food, live entertainment, a celebrity guest host, or someone who's very influential in the community. Give a tour inside the community.

Another thing you need to know when setting your date is that it is convenient to your customers, suppliers and others. You will need to check with the Chamber to determine when the best time is for the Ambassadors. Usually an early evening (around 5:00pm) is best and the Ambassadors prefer the day of the week to be Monday through Thursday. This way, Ambassadors and staff can come straight from work. In addition, you need to allow time to secure and mail invites as well as make other arrangements for your event.

The chamber will also do a ribbon cut and take pictures, having a photographer and videographer is very important. Getting your customers engage is very important, like having a raffles and doing an onsite contest.

When sending out invitations do not clutter the invitation with a lot of pictures or wording. Get the point across in short one-line bullet points. Be sure to mention your business name, address, phone, email, web site, time, date, and place, what the event is, if an RSVP is necessary, call back number, etc. If you are going to serve food and refreshments, you should also mention this. Determine whether or not the event will be catered.

At my grand opening I felt that that hiring a catering company allowed me to focus on my guest. It also gave me credibility of being professional and adding a great presentation to my future clients and staff. One of the universal truths of store grand openings is that they don't just happen. They take planning — and lots of it.

In closing remember that your opening event establishes your relationship with the community, business partners and all who took part in the event. Now that you have taking all precaution to preparing for the grand opening. Create a mailing list from your attendees, to follow up by sending Thank You cards to all who attended, that will keep your event and business fresh in everyone's mind in addition to bringing back memories of the event. This is a great way to solidify your business in the community. My goal for writing this book is to successful help someone. My motto is we can all eat no need to compete. Another person's success does not mean I have less opportunity. In fact, another's success can actually be my success.

I am so thankful for being a part of your process; you have all the ingredients of being a successful entrepreneur. Understand that your network is your net worth. Do not quit, do not give up. Always go back to the drive you had on why you started. God has equipped you for this day. Proverbs 18 vs. 16" Your gift will make room for you and will bring you in front of great men". This business didn't happen by chance it happened because you aligned your actions with the universe and birth your masterpieces. I leave you with this, when you give up it's like slashing your 3 tires because you only have one flat. Stay empowered, obstacles are here to push you into your greatness, looking forwarding to hearing your success story.

No matter the obstacle, know that you will be successful. Your business goals will come to fruition, keep a positive mindset, never give up on your dream. You can achieve what you put your mind on. I want to encourage you to into your destiny, no matter where you start use what you have learned in this book to be successful. Enjoy the ride, set detailed bright goals for your future self. I wish you great victory; I know this book will help you succeed in opening your High-End Boutique. Thank you for your time and support, many blessings to you. Within yourself you have all talents needed to fulfill your dreams!

If you need additional services or coaching, please visit

http://fashionnetworkingnightout.com/Boutique-Coaching

CPSIA information can be obtained
at www.ICGtesting.com
Printed in the USA
LVHW071345191119
637859LV00012B/349/P